Barrier-Free Travel

FAVORITE FLORIDA STATE PARKS
FOR WHEELERS AND SLOW WALKERS

Candy B. Harrington

PHOTOGRAPHS BY
CHARLES PANNELL

CANDY & CHARLES CREATIVE CONCEPTS

ISBN: 978-0-9985103-0-9

Candy & Charles Creative Concepts
PO Box 278
Ripon, CA 95366-0278

To Charles

Contents

Preface
Experience the Real Florida

As we cruised slowly down the St. Johns River, our guide reminded us to keep our eyes peeled for bubbles. Specifically we were on the lookout for trails of circular bubbles interspersed with the occasional group of large gaseous-looking bubbles, as these were signs of manatee activity. Even though it was past prime time for manatees in the area, we were still hopeful.

We were a small group — a man from Arizona, two sisters from Maine, and us. And then Arizona man shouted, "I see bubbles up ahead." A few minutes later a tannin-stained manatee surfaced, just a few feet from our riverboat. We could see the propeller scars on his back — an all too common wound on the animals — and hear him take a deep breath before he dropped back beneath the surface. It was truly one of those "serendipity moments". And then we spotted more bubbles up ahead, and yet another manatee surfaced. We lingered there in silence and watched the enormous animals surface every few minutes, as our guide reminded us that this was the real Florida. "A lot of folks come to Florida for the theme parks," she sighed, "but this is the real Florida experience right here." And I totally agree.

Apparently the folks at Florida State Parks also agree, as their tagline is "The Real Florida".

And we had many of those Real Florida moments as we researched this book in the Sunshine State. They ranged from seeing wild pigs rut right outside our cabin, to hearing male alligators bellow out their eerie mating calls. Then there was the sighting of a baby gator, so small that you knew mama was lurking nearby; and then subsequently seeing another gator gulp up a fish on a previously pristine lake. Our bird sightings included close encounters with egrets, herons, ibis and spoonbills; as well as spying some fluffy little limpkin chicks, and a family of Sandhill Cranes with their feathered-out youngster. And then there was that up-close-and-personal encounter with a Pileated Woodpecker. Top it off with a firefly show that was second-to-none, and you have the Real Florida experience.

The good news is, you don't have to be the Steve Irwin type to experience the Real Florida. And that's the main reason for this book. I figured that lodging would be the biggest obstacle for wheelers and slow walkers who want to spend some time in the state parks, and I was thrilled to find that some Florida State Parks offer fully-equipped cabins. I was even more thrilled to discover that some of them are also wheelchair-accessible — of course their access varies, and to be honest no two are exactly identical. Again, another reason for this book — to describe their access so you can decide what will work best for you. And you'll find lots of photos and detailed access descriptions of the cabins in this book.

Alternatively, if you want to rough it and sleep out under the stars, I've also included some campground information, and even details about a primitive camp site in the Florida Keys that may work for some people. On the other hand, if you're just up for a day trip, and really don't want to overnight in the park, I've included a few parks that are good for a day visit too.

But lodging is just part of the equation, as visitors also have to be able to get out and see the Real Florida, on the trails, boats and tours in the state parks. To be honest I found a fair amount of access information online, but not all of it was factually correct. Upon further investigation I discovered some accessible trails and sites that weren't listed on websites, as well as some sites and tours that were listed as "accessible", that didn't quite make the grade. So, as I do in all of my books, I described the access I found, so you can determine if the trail, tour or boat will work for you. After all, everyone has different access needs.

Finally, I need to point out that this is not a comprehensive guide to all of Florida's state parks — it's a collection of some of my favorites. Truly there were some that we visited that just didn't make the cut either access-wise or content-wise, and those of course were not included. But I do have very specific reasons for including every chosen park, and those reasons are detailed in the book. And as you know, things can change over time, so when I become aware of any changes I'll update them on the book website at www.BarrierFreeFlorida.com. And if you happen to come across a change, I encourage you to let me know so I can share the news with others.

In the end, I encourage you to get out and explore the Real Florida, and I offer this book up as a starting point for your incredible journey. So give it a shot, and let me know what you think. Truly, it's probably more accessible than you imagine.

Candy Harrington

candy@EmergingHorizons.com   Facebook: Candy Harrington
www.CandyHarrington.com   Twitter: Candy B. Harrington
www.EmergingHorizons.com   Pinterest: Candy Harrington

The Basics

Although there's a great diversity of wildlife and terrain throughout Florida state parks, there are some system-wide resources that will not only help you plan your visit, but also save you a few bucks along the way. With that in mind, here are some helpful tips, links and contacts to help you map out a perfectly accessible Sunshine State visit.

Florida State Parks Annual Pass

If you plan to visit a number of Florida state parks, then consider purchasing an individual or family annual pass. The individual pass is good for the passholder only; while the family pass is valid for up to eight people, except at Ellie Schiller Homosassa Springs Wildlife State Park and Weeki Wachee Springs State park, where it's good for up to two people. The passes are valid for one year, and they can be ordered online at the Florida State Parks Store (shop.floridastateparks.org/shop/passes-passports.html), or purchased at any state park entrance. The individual pass is priced at $60, while the family pass costs $120.

Honorably discharged veterans can receive a 25% discount on annual passes, by providing a drivers license and a copy of their DD Form 214 at any park entrance. Additionally, veterans with a service-connected disability can receive a free lifetime pass. Proof of identification, service-connected disability and honorable discharge are required. As with the veterans discount pass, this pass can only be obtained in person.

Disabled Toll Permit

Some disabled individuals may also be eligible for a disabled toll permit, which grants users free access to Florida toll roads that have manned stations. In order to qualify for this permit, you must have a valid driver's license and have an upper limb mobility or dexterity disability that impairs you from tossing coins into toll booth baskets. You must also drive an adapted vehicle in order to be eligible for this permit. There is no charge for the permit, but you must provide a doctor's statement that documents your disability. It takes about six to eight weeks to receive a disabled toll permit, and it's valid for five years. Once you receive the permit, just attach the orange sticker to your window. Then, whenever you pass through a manned toll station the attendant will record your permit number, and you'll be allowed to pass through at no charge. It should be noted that the disabled toll permit is not valid at unmanned stations. Applications for a disabled toll permit can be found at www.dot.state.fl.us/ctd/tollpermit.htm. Questions about the disabled toll permit should be directed to the Florida Commission for the Transportation Disadvantaged at (800) 983-2435.

Sun Pass

Once you receive your disabled toll permit, you are eligible to apply for a Sun Pass non-revenue mini transponder. This small electronic device is permanently attached to a windshield, and allows users to pass through unmanned lanes toll-free. There is a $4.95 fee for the non-revenue mini-transponder, but after the initial purchase you are not required to fill or refill it. Applications for a Sun Pass non-revenue mini transponder can be found at www.dot.state.fl.us/ctd/tollpermit.htm. Questions about this program should be directed to Sun Pass at (561) 488-5312.

Even if you don't qualify for a Sun Pass non-revenue mini transponder, you can still purchase a regular Sun Pass mini transponder, that will allow you to pass through unmanned toll lanes. You can purchase a Sun Pass mini-transponder for $4.99, or a Sun Pass portable transponder for $19.99 at all turnpike service plazas, AAA South offices and over 3,000 retail locations (including Publix and CVS) in Florida. You can find locations that sell the passes, and also purchase them online at www. SunPass.com. Unlike the non-revenue Sun Pass, a $10 minimum initial balance is required to be loaded at the time of activation. Subsequent refills can be made in person or on the Sun Pass website.

Because of the $14.99 minimum initial investment, it pays to find out how much the tolls will run along your scheduled route, to determine if a Sun Pass purchase is cost effective. To calculate the tolls along your route visit www.floridasturnpike.com.

Toll-by-Plate

If you don't opt for a Sun Pass, you can still pass though unmanned lanes thanks to Florida's Toll-by-Plate program. Whenever a car without a Sun Pass transponder passes through an unmanned lane, a photo is taken of the license plate, and the registered owner is sent an invoice (not a fine) about a month later. You can then either mail in a check or pay the invoice online. A $2.50 administrative fee is also added to the toll charges. It should be noted that Sun Pass users save approximately 33% over Toll-by-Plate users, but again if you don't plan on doing much turnpike driving, Toll-by-Plate may be the more economical option. Currently the Toll-by-Plate program is available on the Homestead Extension of Florida's Turnpike, from Florida City to Miramar. For more information on Toll-by-Plate, visit www.tollbyplate.com.

Camping

A 50% discount on Florida State Park campsites is available to Florida citizens who are at least 65 years old, and to Florida citizens who have a current social security disability award certificate or a 100% disability award certificate from the federal government. Proof of age, residency and disability are required upon arrival. This discount is not available on cabins.

Campsite reservations can be made up to 11 months in advance through ReserveAmerica at www.floridastateparks.reserveamerica.com, or by calling (800) 326-3521.

Weather & Road Conditions

Information about traffic congestion, road construction and accidents on Florida roads can be found at www.fl511.com. You can also view traffic web cams and read the most recent traffic alerts on this website. Traffic information can also be obtained by dialing 511 throughout the state.

Information about Florida state park closures, traffic congestion and other alerts can be found at www.floridastateparks.org.

Florida is divided into two separate weather zones. The south part of the state boasts pleasant weather and mild temperatures during the peak tourist season, from December to March. During the summer, visitation tends to fall off in this part of the state because of the high temperatures and heavy rainfall, especially in July and August. On the other hand, the northern part of the state experiences peak season in summer because of milder temperatures. April (outside of Easter week) through May, and September through November are considered the shoulder seasons. During this time, the weather is still nice, lodging prices are a bit lower, and the tourist crowds are pleasantly absent. It should also be noted that some concessions in the state parks operate on reduced hours or close entirely during the shoulder seasons, so check in advance to avoid disappointment. Additionally, hurricane season runs from June through November.

Vultures

Over the past five years vultures have become an increasing problem in Florida. And although they are fun to watch and photograph, they also pose a huge threat to vehicles. During the winter months these massive birds have been know to destroy the rubber trim, windshield wipers and sun roof seals of vehicles parked near the water. A few places — such as the Royal Palm Visitor Center in Everglades National Park — even post warning signs and provide visitors with protective tarps to cover their vehicles. Be on the lookout for groups of vultures in any parking areas, and park in the sun if possible. Additionally, if you plan to visit a lot of places near the water during the winter, you might want to invest in an inexpensive car cover, especially if you have a sun roof.

Florida State Park Resources

www.FloridaStateParks.org
www.twitter.com/FLStateParks
www.facebook.com/FLStateParks

Manatee Springs State Park

L ocated in Northwest Florida, about six miles west of Chiefland,
Manatee Springs State Park is home to a first-magnitude spring that
produces over 100 million gallons of crystal clear water each day The spring
run meanders through a hardwood wetland area and empties into the
nearby Suwannee River. During the winter months, West Indian manatees
swim upriver from the colder Gulf of Mexico to seek out the warmer waters
of Manatee Springs. During this winter migration, visitors can get an up-
close-and-personal look at these gentle giants from the beach or boardwalk
areas of the park. And if that's not reason enough to visit Manatee Springs,
the manatee viewing areas are also nicely accessible — a pertinent detail
that's unfortunately been omitted from the park's collateral materials.

Attractions

Day Use Area

There's plenty of accessible parking in the day use lot, with a level sidewalk
over to the concession building. There's ramp access up to the snack bar,
which serves up BBQ ribs, chicken, and pulled pork plates, plus hot dogs,
snacks, ice cream and cold drinks.

Boardwalk at Manatee Springs State Park

A large accessible family restroom is located next door. It features a full five-foot turning radius and is equipped with a roll-under sink and an accessible toilet with grab bars.

If you'd prefer to pack along your lunch, there's a large picnic area behind the concession building. A few accessible picnic tables are located under the trees, and there's level access to the picnic shelters. And although not all of the picnic tables are accessible, they are located on level ground, so some wheelchair-users may still be able to roll up beside them to eat.

There's level access over to an accessible boardwalk, just to the left of the concession area. This nicely done pathway meanders over a cypress swamp, and has benches and interpretive plaques along the way. It's shaded by the trees, so it's a good spot to escape the midday sun, and enjoy the view of the lovely blue-green crystal clear waters. The quarter-mile boardwalk ends at a dock on the Suwannee River, which has a few benches and a shade cover. Ranger-led programs are often conducted on the boardwalk, so be sure and check at the ranger station for a current program schedule.

There's also a cement boat ramp near the beginning of the boardwalk, that could conceivably be used to access the water for a swim. In order to protect the manatees, motorized boat traffic is prohibited at Manatee Springs, so the boat ramp is now used as a canoe launch.

Another boardwalk is located on the other side of the swimming area. This short trail leads over to a hard-packed dirt trail out to the beach. There's ramp access from the beach down into the water, and there are also a few standard picnic tables in a level dirt area nearby. Although the tables aren't technically accessible, they are doable for many people, as there's plenty of room to roll up alongside them.

North End Trail

Although it's not rated as accessible, some wheelchair-users and slow walkers may be able to navigate this 2.5-mile loop trail. Pick up a trail guide at the ranger station, and look for the dirt road to the trailhead, just past the park entrance on the right. There's no designated parking, but there's rarely any cars in the level dirt parking area.

There are three trailheads located near the parking area. One leads down to the day use area, and one goes back to the ranger station. The third trailhead – which is marked "scenic trail" — is the beginning of the North End Trail self-guided nature walk. This hard-packed dirt trail is fairly level, but there are patches of sand along the route, which may be problematic for manual wheelchair-users. That said, it's a good choice for most power wheelchair-users, scooter-users, and even some slow walkers. And if you can't manage the whole length of the trail, just turn around when you think you've had enough.

For the most part the trail is covered in duff, and it passes through a beautiful cypress, palmetto and magnolia covered woodland area. Near the halfway point, there's a replica of a Seminole chickee hut. This shelter, which was erected to honor the park's heritage, has level access on three sides, and a raised sleeping platform in the back. It's a fitting tribute, and a perfectly pleasant place to enjoy a picnic lunch.

It should be noted that the last half-mile of the trail may not be doable for some folks. At this point the trail narrows and cuts through the forest. It's still pretty level, but because of the proximity of the trees, there are exposed roots along this section of the trail. Still, most of the obstructions are easy to dodge, and many people won't have any problems. The best part about this section of the trail is that the dense forest provides some welcome shade. It should also be noted that this trail totally loses any access it has after a rain storm, as it turns into a muddy mess. Still, in dry weather it's a very nice nature walk.

North End Trail at Manatee Springs State Park

Lodging

Magnolia 1 Campground

The Magnolia 1 Campground, which is located near the day use area, is the newest and most accessible campground in the park.

Campsites 20 and 32 are accessible tent sites. Both sites are paved and have raised grills, and they include level concrete paths to the nearby bathhouse. Site 32 has an accessible picnic table, while site 20 has a standard picnic table.

Campsites 7 and 40 are accessible RV or trailer sites. These pull-through sites are paved and they each have a raised grill and an accessible picnic table. There is also an accessible concrete path to the bathhouse from both sites.

Campsites 5 and 26 are also designated as accessible on the ReserveAmerica site, most likely because they are near the bathhouse; however they both have gravel driveways. Campsite 5 is a pull through RV site and campsite 26 is a tent site.

The bathhouse has a large family restroom with a wide door and a full five-foot turning radius. It's equipped with a roll-in shower with a hand-held showerhead, grab bars and a fold-down shower seat. Other access features include a roll-under sink and toilet grab bars. There is also barrier-free access to the men's and women's restrooms, which both have accessible stalls.

Hickory Campground

Hickory Campground is located across the street from the Magnolia 1 Campground. Campsites 76 and 77 are accessible RV or trailer sites. They are located across from the bathhouse and they both are paved and have raised grills and accessible tables. It should be noted that site 77 is not designated as accessible on the ReserveAmerica site. Additionally these sites are labeled as sites 11 and 12 on some park campground maps.

There is level access to the bathhouse. Both the men's and women's side have a roll-in shower with grab bars and a hand-held showerhead. Other access features include roll-under sinks, toilet grab bars and portable shower chairs.

Resources

Manatee Springs State Park
(352) 493-6072
www.floridastateparks.org/park/manatee-springs

Replica of a Seminole chickee hut on the North End Trail

Fanning Springs State Park

L ocated about 20 minutes from Manatee Springs State Park, Fanning Springs produces less than 65 million gallons of water a day, so technically it's classified as a second-magnitude spring. Still it's a lovely state park, with plenty of opportunities for manatee watching during the winter months. But truly the best part of the park is the accessible cabin, and the peace and quiet. There's no campground in the park, and there are only five cabins, so after the day visitors depart, you can hear a pin drop. Additionally, the cabin host's RV is parked right next to the cabins, so that also helps keep the noise level very low. Plus you just can't beat the firefly show from the cabin's screened porch. In short, it's Mother Nature at her finest.

Attractions

Day Use Area

There's plenty of accessible parking in the day use lot, with level access over to the concession building. Alternatively there's a level hard-packed dirt trial that leads from the cabin area to the day use area. It's about 100 yards long and doable for most wheelchair-users and slow walkers.

Boardwalk at Fanning Springs State Park

There's level access from the parking lot to the picnic area, which features some accessible tables on hard-packed dirt under a grove of trees. There's also level access to the covered picnic shelter.

A sidewalk leads from the parking lot to the concession building, where the snack bar serves up barbecue chicken, rib and pulled pork plates, as well as hot dogs, cold drinks and ice cream. An accessible restroom is located near the snack bar.

A paved pathway begins next to the concession area and leads down to the swimming area, however there is only stairway access down to the water. Alternatively some wheelchair-users may be able to access the water from the nearby boat dock, which serves as the canoe launch site.

To the left of the swimming area there is level access to an observation deck, which was formerly a diving platform. And to the right there's a beautiful accessible boardwalk that winds through the cypress swamp for a quarter-mile to a shaded pavilion. It's s nice stroll, and you'll probably see a mullet fish or two jump out of the blue-green water along the way. The boardwalk is shaded by the vegetation, and there are several benches along the way to sit and take a rest. And if you'd like to learn about the native flora and fauna, there are also a number of interpretive plaques along the boardwalk.

Palmetto Path Nature Trail

The Palmetto Path Nature Trail may also be doable for some wheelchair-users and slow walkers. The trailhead is located near the picnic area, and the 2/3-mile loop winds through the forest and past the cabins. The hard-packed dirt trail can also be accessed between cabin 3 and the cabin host's RV, however there is one large root near the trailhead. Still if you can make it past that obstacle, you're good to go, as the rest of the trail is relatively free from obstructions. It's a short pleasant walk, and also a great stroller trail. As an added bonus, there's usually not much traffic along this trail.

Wayside Picnic Area

There's also a Wayside Picnic Area located off of Highway 19, just west of the park entrance. You can't get to this corner of the park from the other areas of the park, but it's definitely worth the short drive.

There's accessible parking near the picnic area, with curb-cut access to the sidewalk which leads over to a shaded picnic grove. The cement

The Wayside Picnic Area

picnic tables have immovable cement benches, but there's plenty of room for wheelchair seating at the ends. There's also level access over to the picnic shelter, and to a number of benches strategically placed throughout the grove. Accessible restrooms are located across from the picnic area, with barrier-free access from the parking lot. And right behind the restrooms you can get a glance at a section of the Old Fanning Springs Bridge, that used to traverse the Suwannee River.

On the other side of the parking lot, there's a steep ramp down to a floating dock, where you might get a glimpse of a manatee or two in the winter. Manual wheelchair-users may need some assistance because of the grade, but it's a better alternative than the nearby steps. It's also important to note that swimming is not allowed in this area because of the swift current and the alligators.

Lodging

Cabin 4

Accessible cabin 4 is located just a short drive from the park entrance. There's accessible parking in front, with level access to the sidewalk which leads to the zero-step front cabin entrance. This two-bedroom cabin boasts excellent access, and can sleep up to six people.

Inside there's good pathway access over the tile and laminate floors, and plenty of room to maneuver a wheelchair or scooter. The homey cabin is decorated with nature photographs, and has lots of personal touches, and it definitely doesn't feel like a rental.

The great room is furnished with a love seat and a 12-inch high sleeper sofa, a dining table and four chairs, and three tall chairs at the bar. The well-equipped kitchen features a roll-under cooktop (a feature you don't often see), as well as a roll-under sink. It also has a separate oven, a microwave, a full-size refrigerator, a coffee maker and a toaster. And there's a huge closet full of cookware and lots of plates, cups, glasses and utensils. There's also a back door from the kitchen, with level access to the wrap around screened porch.

Cabin 4 at Fanning Springs State Park

The bathroom includes a full five-foot turning radius and is equipped with a roll-in shower with grab bars, a hand-held showerhead and a fold-down shower seat. The toilet grab bars are located on the right and back walls (as seated), and the bathroom also has a roll-under sink. Round it out with a small chest of drawers and you have a very functional bathroom.

One bedroom is furnished with a 25-inch high queen-sized bed with wheelchair access on the left side (as you face it). The other bedroom has two 23-inch high twin beds with an access aisle between them. Both rooms also have a chest of drawers and lowered clothing rods.

By far the best feature of the cabin is the large wrap around screened porch. It's furnished with an accessible picnic table, a swing, three rocking chairs and a small side table. And for added comfort on warm evenings it's also equipped with ceiling fans. There's also level access to a small cement patio behind the cabin with a picnic table and a charcoal grill.

To say that the access is very nicely done in this cabin is an understatement. As one former guest put it, "This is the most accessible state park cabin that I've ever seen." That pretty much sums it up.

Wrap around screened porch at Cabin 4

Bedroom with queen-sized bed in Cabin 4

Bathroom in Cabin 4

Living and dining area in Cabin 4

Kitchen in Cabin 4

Nature Coast State Trail

Although it's not located in the park, the Nature Coast State Trail, which is just across the street from Fanning Springs State Park, is also worth a stop while you're in the area. This 32-mile multiuse trail is paved, fairly level, and is an excellent choice for wheelers and slow walkers. The Fanning Springs trailhead is the hub of the trail, and from there you can set out in whatever direction tickles your fancy.

The Fanning Springs trailhead is located on Highway 19, right behind The Barb-B-Que Shack and Tele-Tech. Parking is available on a level grass area, with level access over to the trail. Alternatively, you can turn down Florida Street (just west of The Barb-B-Que Shack) and park in the Fort Fanning site parking lot, near the intersection of Florida and Lake Streets. This small paved lot has an accessible parking space, with level access out to the trail.

The west branch of the trail terminates in Cross City 12 miles down the road, and features some beautiful views of the Suwannee River along the way. If you want to get away from the crowds, then take the east branch of the trail 7 miles to Trenton. And last but certainly not least, the south section of the trail skirts a beautiful hardwood hammock for 9 miles, before it terminates in Chiefland. And if you can't manage the whole distance of these branches, then set out in your favorite direction and do as much as you can. Even better, bring along your handcycle and do the whole trail.

Resources

Fanning Springs State Park
(352) 463-3420
www.floridastateparks.org/park/Fanning-Springs

Nature Coast State Trail
www.traillink.com/trail/nature-coast-state-trail.aspx

Ellie Schiller Homosassa Springs Wildlife State Park

Homosassa Springs Wildlife Park

Formerly an exotic animal park, this 210-acre compound slowly morphed into a wildlife refuge, before it could be transitioned into the award-winning state park that it is today. Now an exclusive refuge for Florida native species (except for one hippopotamus with some clout), Ellie Schiller Homosassa Springs Wildlife State Park is also home to a first-magnitude crystal clear spring and the Homosassa River headwaters. Add in the three resident manatees, and you have one of the few places in the world where you can see these magnificent creatures year-round.

Located about 175 miles south of Florida's capital city, the park actually has two entrances — an east entrance and a west entrance — with pontoon boat and tram transportation between the two. There's no lodging in the park, but since it's just a short hour-drive from Fanning Springs, it's a very doable day trip. Best of all, it's the perfect place for an introduction to the diverse wildlife of the Sunshine State, as you can see, interact and learn about all of the native species in just one afternoon.

Attractions

Visitor Centers

The east entrance of the park is located on Suncoast Boulevard, just south of West Grover Cleveland Boulevard. There's plenty of accessible parking in the large lot, with level access over to the visitor center. Inside, there's barrier-free access to the ticket counter, gift shop and the accessible restrooms. And although there are steps down to the boarding area for the pontoon boat to the west entrance, there's also elevator access to it. Additionally, there's level access to a picnic shelter with accessible tables outside.

The west entrance, which offers direct access to the compound, is located on West Fishbowl Drive, near the intersection of West Spring Cove Road. Accessible parking is located near the entrance with barrier-free access to the visitor center. There's also level access to the building from the nearby boat dock. There's plenty of room to navigate a wheelchair inside the visitor center with level access to the Wildside Cafe, the ticket counter, the gift shop and the accessible restrooms. Loaner wheelchairs are also available at this entrance.

Pontoon Boat

The pontoon boat departs from the East Visitor Center, and travels 1.2 miles along Pepper Creek to the main compound entrance at the West Visitor Center. There's level access from the dock to the boat at both entrances, with plenty of space in the front of the boat for a wheelchair. The 20-minute ride is included with park admission, and even though there are other ways to get to the compound entrance, it's really a must-do for visitors. During the ride, park rangers share information about the history of the park, as well as point out wildlife and vegetation on the way. You'll spot turtles, ducks and alligators in the tree-lined creek; and if you time it right you might even catch a coveted glimpse of the adult osprey tending to their offspring in a nest near the west entrance.

Fish Bowl

Located near the compound entrance, the aptly named Fish Bowl underwater observatory offers an entirely different view of the resident manatees. Hopes are high that funds can be raised to replace the cloudy and scratched windows which line the lower level of the 50-year old floating dock; but until that happens, you can actually get a better view of the manatees from the accessible viewing area up on top. Additionally,

Boarding ramp for the pontoon boat at Homossasa Springs

there are stairs down to the lower level of this vintage attraction, which makes it a no-go for wheelchair-users and many slow walkers. On the upside, they have installed a monitor on the top level that displays the feed from a camera in the underwater observatory, so wheelchair-users can also get a glimpse of the action.

Park rangers conduct daily manatee education programs from the bleacher area across the pond from the Fish Bowl. There's plenty of room for wheelchair seating in front of the bleachers, but you can also get a view from the cement deck above the Fish Bowl.

Discovery Center

If you have kids in tow, the Discovery Center, which is located a short roll from the Fish Bowl, is a required stop. There's level access to the building, and plenty of room inside to maneuver a wheelchair around the tables filled with puzzles, stamp pads, crayons and other hands-on activities to help youngsters learn about the native animals. You can also get a partial view of the bromeliads in the attached greenhouse from inside, but there's a much better vantage point behind the building. There's also an accessible restroom in the Discovery Center, and a ranger on duty to answer questions.

Garden of the Springs

The Garden of the Springs picnic area, located directly behind the Discovery Center, is the perfect place for a lunch stop. There's level access to a large shelter with several accessible picnic tables, right across from the turtle enclosure. There are also some accessible picnic tables under the tress on hard-packed dirt, and a ramp up to a small pavilion with a few benches. An accessible viewing platform is located near the large picnic shelter, and from there you can take the accessible shaded boardwalk along the river and over the bridge on the manatee pool, to the deer, hippopotamus and alligator enclosures.

Alligator and Hippopotamus Program

Try and time your visit so you can catch the daily alligator and hippopotamus program. There's no official seating for the program, so folks usually just line up around the enclosures around show time. There's level access to the best viewing area, along the cement bridge that separates the hippopotamus enclosure from the alligator lagoon. The show is very informative, and it casts some light on the behaviors and habits of these often misunderstood animals.

And just in case you are wondering, hippos are not indigenous to Florida; in fact Lu (short for Lucifer) is the only non-native species in the park. Born in 1960 at the San Diego Zoo, Lu starred in a number of Hollywood productions including *Tarzan* and *Daktari*. He was also a resident of the old exotic animal park, and a local favorite. After the park changed hands it was announced that Lu had to be relocated because of his "non-native" status. A massive letter writing campaign was then quickly launched by Lu's local fan base. This subsequently caught the attention of then-governor Lawton Chiles, who signed a declaration that made Lu an honorary citizen of Florida and allowed him to stay in the park. Today, he's the oldest living hippopotamus in captivity, and still a local favorite.

Wildlife Walk

By far the highlight of the park is the Wildlife Walk, where rescued and habituated native animals are housed in enclosures along the north portion of the park's 1.1-miles of accessible boardwalks and walkways. There are

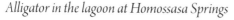

Alligator in the lagoon at Homossasa Springs

interpretive panels in front of the enclosures filled with barn owls, red wolfs, great horned owls, black bears, alligators and crocodiles. There's also a nice collection of wading birds in the ponds that line the boardwalk — including a bevy of flamingoes — and a good assortment other Florida avian life in the aviary. Access is excellent throughout the Wildlife Walk with level pathways, barrier-free access to the aviary and reptile house, and plenty of good vantage points for wheelchair-users. There's also an accessible restroom located near the bear enclosure. This diverse collection not only offers a good primer on Florida wildlife, but also educates folks on ecology and conservation efforts in the Sunshine State.

Pepper Creek Trail

When you're ready to leave the park, you can either take the boat back, hop on the tram or walk back to the east entrance on the Pepper Creek Trail.

Although the boat is nice, the tram offers an entirely different view of the area, as it travels along the .75-mile Pepper Creek Trail. There's barrier-free access over to the tram boarding area from the west entrance, and the tram itself is wheelchair-accessible.

Alternatively you can walk along the level paved trail. It's quite pleasant as it's shaded by the forest canopy, and there are benches to stop

Begining of the Wildlife Walk at Homossasa Springs

and rest along the way. Part of the Great Florida Birding Trail, this route is especially popular in the fall and spring, when you can spot migratory warblers, vireos and thrushes along the way.

Resources

Ellie Schiller Homosassa Springs Wildlife State Park
(352) 628-5343
www.floridastateparks.org/park/Homosassa-Springs

Pepper Creek Trail at Homossasa Springs

Weeki Wachi Springs State Park

To say that Weeki Wachi Springs is a classic Florida attraction is a bit of an understatement. Established in 1946 by dive instructor Newton Perry, this old school theme park focused on the basics — pretty girls and the natural beauty of a first-magnitude spring. Perry constructed an 18-seat underwater theater and taught his mermaids to swim and breath through air hoses and flash enticing siren-like smiles at the audience. It was a hit on all levels.

The American Broadcasting Company knew a good thing when they saw it, so they purchased the park in 1959. A larger theater was subsequently constructed, and with strong promotion from the network, this family-friendly park continued to enjoy a heyday well into the next decade. Unfortunately with the development of the mega theme parks, the appeal of simpler down-to-earth attractions like Weeki Wachi faded. In 2008 it was converted to a state park, and today the mermaids still "work their tails off" at this iconic Florida attraction. And although there are no overnight accommodations in the park, a day visit to this Spring Hill attraction is a must-do for anyone who wants to turn back the clock and enjoy a taste of old Florida.

Attractions

Entry Plaza

There's plenty of accessible parking near the entrance, and level access to the park from the fountain side of the entrance plaza. Once inside the park, there's level access to the spring overlook on the right, and the gift shop and information center on the left. Accessible restrooms are located next to the gift shop. From the entry plaza there's barrier-free access to both the original mermaid-themed park, as well as the Buccaneer Bay water park addition.

It should be noted that Weeki Wachee is extremely popular on weekends, holidays and during the summer. During this time admission is capacity controlled, and once the maximum number of guests are admitted, the gates are closed until space for new guests has been made. The park opens at 9:00 a.m., so it's best to arrive by 8:30 a.m. in order to guarantee admission during the peak season. It should also be noted that even guests that have tickets and annual pass holders are subject to these admission rules.

Underwater Theater

The mermaid show, which takes place in the underwater theater, is the highlight of any Weeki Wachee visit. It's a definite hit with the little ones, and a nice walk down memory lane for the rest of us.

There's level access over to the theater entrance, near the spring overlook; and although the ramp into the theater is a bit on the steep side, there's a large contingent of ushers available to assist folks who can't manage the grade. Seating is available in bleacher-type seats with backs, with five steps down to the last row of seats. Wheelchair and companion seating is available behind the last row, and because of the setup of the theater, these seats also offer a good line of sight. And if you just can't manage the steps to the bleacher seats, let an usher know, and they will set up folding chairs for your party in the wheelchair section.

The underwater theater is pretty much like it sounds. Large windows grace the front of the theater, and when the curtains are pulled back guests are treated to a fun show with the mermaids, fish and turtles in the lagoon. Top that off with the occasional appearance of a cast member on stage, and some vintage clips of mermaids in training, and you have a very entertaining production.

And if you'd like a bite to eat after the show, the Mermaid Galley

Mermaids perform at the Weeki Wachee Underwater Theater

Restaurant is located just a short walk from the underground theater. There's level access to the restaurant, which serves up a variety of salads, sandwiches and grill items. There's also barrier-free access to the nearby Captains Quarters, which offers some tasty ice cream treats to top off your meal. Accessible restrooms are located across from the Mermaid Galley Restaurant.

Discovery Point

Don't miss the daily wildlife shows at the Discovery Point Theater, which can be accessed by the Tranquility Trail. Although some wheelchair-users may need assistance at the beginning of the trail, the grade levels out after the first patch. The hard-packed trail is covered in stabalized limestone, and winds through the forest canopy and over a boardwalk to the outdoor Discovery Point Theater.

There's level access to the theater which features bleacher seating. Wheelchair seats are available in front of the first row, with companion seats behind them. The wildlife show features a yellow bellied slider and a juvenile alligator, and offers an educational and entertaining look at these, and many other, Florida natives.

And for a closer look at Florida wildlife, save some time for a

Alligator in the wildlife show at the Discovery Point Theatre

39

wilderness river cruise on the *Aqua Belle*. There's level access to the boarding area, which is located near the Tranquility Trail trailhead. There's lift access down to the boat, and wheelchair-users can stay in their own wheelchair for the entire calm water cruise. The one-mile cruise travels down the winding river, as the captain points out wildlife along the way. The pontoon boat is also covered, which is a big plus in the afternoon.

Buccaneer Bay

There's a barrier-free pathway to Buccaneer Bay, which is located on the other side of the lagoon. This water park attraction was added in 1982, and although the three water slides are not wheelchair-accessible, it's still worth a visit if you'd like to take a dip in the lagoon. Best of all, there's no extra charge to visit the water park.

A level sidewalk leads over to a ramp which offers direct access down to the water. Granted you'll need to bring your own water wheelchair, or you need to be able to walk with assistance to get into the water, but the ramp at least makes it doable. As an added bonus, the spring water is crystal clear, so you'll also get a good look at the fish. And if you just want to sit back and enjoy the beach, there's level access to a sandy beach with lounge chairs, as well as a nearby shaded patio area.

Ramped access to the water at Buccaneer Bay

There are three picnic areas near the beach, all of which are located on a level grassy area and have accessible picnic tables. There is also ramp access up to the sundeck. The Pirate Grub and Snack Shack concession areas offer barrier-free access, and there's an accessible restroom and changing area located between them. And if you'd like to enjoy an adult beverage, there's ramp access up to the Tiki Bar, which overlooks the beach.

Resources

Weeki Wachi Springs State Park
(352) 592-5689
www.weekiwachee.com

Myakka River State Park

Located just outside of Sarasota proper, Myakka River State Park is known as the place where the river and prairie meet the sky. Indeed the diversity of the landscape is reason enough to visit Florida's largest state park; however there's also a huge historical component to the site — one that dates back to 1934. It was in that year that President Roosevelt's Civilian Conservation Corps (CCC) began construction on five log cabins near the main park entrance.

Today these CCC cabins have stood the test of time, even though a few creature comforts have been added over the years. And although wheelchair access wasn't even on the radar when they were originally constructed, thanks to some recent renovations, wheelchair-users and slow walkers can now overnight in one of these historic structures.

Attractions

Visitor Center

The main park entrance is located just off of Highway 72, nine miles east of I-75. Although the majority of park visitors can just drive through the entrance kiosk after paying their fees, folks that have cabin reservations need to step inside the ranger station to register.

The best place to park is in the visitor center parking lot, which offers plenty of accessible parking. It's just a short level roll over to the ranger station, which boasts barrier-free access and a lowered check-in counter. There's also level access to the visitor center, which features a variety of interpretive exhibits and a nice selection of movies about the flora and fauna of the area. Accessible restrooms are located in the visitor center.

The Log Pavilion picnic area is also located near the main entrance, a short drive from the visitor center. It features accessible parking, and level access over to picnic tables on a shaded platform. There are also accessible picnic tables under the trees in a level dirt area.

River Walk

The seven-mile park road runs from the main entrance station up to the north entrance, and passes through wetlands, prairies, hammocks and pinelands along the way. There are several places to stop on the drive for a closer look at the different habitats in the park. The first stop you'll come to as you drive north is the River Walk trail, which is located on the right side of the road just after you cross the first bridge.

There's a large circular parking lot, but no real visible signage from the road. The lot is paved, but there are no designated accessible spots. There's level access over to the trailhead, which is located by the interpretive sign near the back of the parking area.

The hard-packed dirt trail is mainly level, and it parallels the river for most of its length. There is a second trail which branches off to the left near the trailhead, but it's filled with roots and other obstructions and not accessible at all.

The main trail winds through a hammock, and until it gets close to the river it's relatively free of obstructions. As the trail turns towards the river, it becomes increasingly more impassable because of tree roots. It's a pleasant walk, and doable for some folks, so give it a try, as you can always turn back if it becomes too rough. It's also a good idea to keep an eye out for alligators as you approach the river, as they're not uncommon in this habitat.

River Walk in Myakka River State Park

William S. Boylston Nature Trail

The William S. Boylston Nature Trail, which is located up the road, is one of the more accessible trails in the park. There's accessible parking in the small lot, with level access over to the nature trail on the left, and the Canopy Walkway (which isn't wheelchair-accessible) on the right.

The .8-mile loop nature trail winds through a shady hardwood forest, and the hard-packed dirt trail transitions into two boardwalk sections across marsh areas along the way. There is about a one-inch lip at the beginning of each boardwalk section, and although some wheelchair-users might need a bit of assistance, it's probably the biggest obstacle along the trail. There are a few tree roots along the dirt section, but since the trail is wide they are pretty easy to dodge. There are also some benches along the way, if you'd like to take a break.

And for a nice lunch break, head over to the small picnic area across the main park road, just south of the nature trail. It's not on any of the park maps but it features accessible parking and barrier-free access to an accessible table on a cement slab.

William S. Boylston Nature Trail in Myakka River State Park

Myakka Outpost

Myakka Outpost, which is the main concession area in the park, is located mid-way along the main park road. There's lots of accessible parking near the building entrance, with ramped access to the second floor of the stilted structure. There's barrier-free access to the Pink Gator cafe which offers a good selection of subs, salads and burgers; and level access over to Myakka Gifts & Boutique which features souvenirs, camp supplies, ice, firewood, books and works by local artists. Accessible restrooms are also located on the second floor.

There is a shaded picnic area across from Myakka Outpost, and level access to a covered pavilion with accessible picnic tables. There's also a short hard-packed dirt trail out to the weir from the far end of the parking lot. It's a nice place to get a view of the wading birds that frequent the area, and if you'd like to drop your line, there's also an accessible fishing area.

Additional accessible parking is available in front of Myakka Outfitters, down at the other end of the complex. There are three steps up to this camp store, and although there was once a wheelchair ramp in the back, it was washed away in the floods. Still it's a great place to park if all the spots in front of Myakka Outpost are taken.

Airboat tour boarding dock in Myakka River State Park

Airboat Tour

Airboat tours on the *Myakka Maiden* or the *Gator Gal* depart several times a day from the dock next to Myakka Outpost. There's level access to the ticket booth and out to the adjacent dock, and ramped access down into the boat. Although the ramp may be a bit steep for some wheelchair-users, assistance is available. There's also a small three-inch step down into the boat that may require assistance. Still the crew is very adept at assisting passengers, and once aboard, wheelchair-users can stay in their own wheelchairs for the whole cruise.

This is definitely a wildlife tour, so it's best to go early in the day when the animals are more active. Expect to see a lot of alligators at that time, as well as osprey on the prowl for food. And if you're lucky, you'll also spot some bald eagles out near the birdwalk. The captain offers a good interpretation of the native wildlife, and pulls up near shore for a closer look whenever possible. It's an excellent way to get a good overview of the residents of Myakka Lake.

Safari Tram Tour

If you'd prefer a history-based tour on the park roads that are closed to vehicle traffic, then sign up for a Safari Tram Tour. Tickets can be purchased at the airboat ticket booth, and guests receive a 50% discount on the Safari Tram Tour if they also book an airboat tour. It should be noted that although the tour is accessible, the operator needs about a half-hour advance notice in order to reconfigure the tram for a wheelchair.

The tram boarding area is located next to the dock in a large flat dirt area. The first car in the open-air tram can be configured for a wheelchair-user, by removing the bench seat and positioning the portable ramp next to the car. Wheelchair-users can roll right on to the tram, and companion seats are available in an adjacent area.

There's another set of restrooms near the boarding area, and although they are ramped they don't have any accessible stalls; so plan ahead and use the accessible restrooms at Myakka Outpost.

The tour focuses on the history of early Florida settlers as the tram travels through an oak and palm forest. Although not primarily a wildlife tour, you'll probably at least catch a gander of a baby gator or two, or maybe even a soft-shell turtle in the swampy ditch alongside the road. The road does get a bit bumpy in a few places, but if you can handle that, it's a good way to access some of the historic back roads in the park.

Birdwalk

Many visitors only make it as far as Myakka Outpost, which is unfortunate because the very accessible birdwalk is located a short drive north of the concession area. There's a small parking lot with an accessible parking space, and barrier-free access over to the birdwalk. The boardwalk trail features level access out over the marsh to the lake's edge. And if you'd like to sit and linger a bit, there's a bench at the end of the line. It's a great place to spot wading birds, and the site is also frequented by the resident bald eagles.

Clay Gully Picnic Area

The Clay Gully Picnic Area, which is located near the north entrance, is a good choice for a secluded picnic, as it's probably the quietest picnic area in the park. There's no signage for it — hence the seclusion — so if you're going north on the park road take the first right after you cross Clay Gully Creek. The winding road widens out to a level parking area under the trees where there are a few picnic tables. Although the tables aren't technically

Birdwalk trail in Myakka River State Park

accessible, and there's no designated parking, the area is level and fairly easy to navigate in a wheelchair. One table over by the creek offers a particularly scenic, if not somewhat isolated, vantage point.

If you'd prefer a slightly less rustic picnic area, the loop road continues on to a large paved lot with accessible parking near the restrooms. There's barrier-free access to a picnic shelter with accessible tables and grills, as well as to a lone picnic table on the grass under the trees. And although there's barrier-free access to the restroom, there are no accessible stalls, so plan ahead and stop at Myakka Outpost beforehand.

Lodging

Cabin 1

The CCC cabins are located a short drive from the ranger station, near the south park entrance, but off the main park road. Crafted from cabbage palm logs chinked together with tar and sawdust, the cabins are surrounded by a pine and palm forest, which not only gives visitors an added layer of privacy, but also offers up some prime wildlife viewing opportunities.

Cabin 1 in Myakka River State Park

There's plenty of room to park an accessible van in the large level area in front of Cabin 1, with level access over to a ramp which leads up to the front door of the raised cabin. Inside there's barrier-free access throughout the cabin, as well as hardwood flooring that makes for easy rolling. The compact kitchen includes a microwave, stove, coffee maker, toaster and a full-size refrigerator; and it's outfitted with a full compliment of dishes, utensils and cookware.

The adjacent great room is furnished with a dining table and six chairs, a 14-inch high futon, two 26-inch high open-framed double beds with an access aisle between them, a bedside table, a wardrobe and a chest of drawers.

The spacious bathroom includes a full five-foot turning radius, and is equipped with a 36-inch square roll-in shower with grab bars, a hand-held showerhead and a fold-down shower bench. The toilet grab bars are located on the left and back walls (as seated), and the bathroom also includes a roll-under sink.

And although the cabin is rustic, a small air conditioner and a heater have been added. Top it off with the original stone fireplace and you have everything you need to keep you warm and toasty.

Out back there's an accessible picnic table and a grill, and although

Living space in Cabin 1

there are three steps down from the back porch, the picnic area is accessible from the front parking area. The cabin also features a nice back deck that borders the woods, so make sure to pack along some lawn chairs so you can fully enjoy it.

The spacious cabin sleeps six and it's a great option for a family getaway. Reservations can be made up to 11 months in advance, but plan ahead to avoid disappointment, as space fills up quickly, especially during holidays and on weekends.

Sleeping space in Cabin 1

Bathroom in Cabin 1

Kitchen in Cabin 1

Palmetto Ridge Campground

Palmetto Ridge Campground is located near the cabins and it offers four accessible sites.

Sites 61 and 63 are located near the first bathhouse. Site 61 is a RV or trailer site, while 63 is a RV or tent site. Each site has a paved driveway with an accessible picnic table, and features an accessible paved pathway to the bathhouse. The men's and women's bathhouses both feature ramp access and have a roll-in shower with grab bars, a lowered showerhead and a fold-down shower bench. Each bathhouse is also equipped with an accessible toilet stall and a roll-under sink.

Sites 76 and 84 are RV or tent sites, and they are located near the second bathhouse. They offer the same access features as the other Palmetto Ridge accessible sites, and the second bathhouse includes the same access features as the first bathhouse.

Big Flat Campground

Big Flat Campground is located near Myakka Outpost and it offers one accessible RV or trailer site. There's lots of shade in this campground, and the trees also offer an added level of privacy between the sites.

Site 6 features a cement pad and an accessible picnic table. It also has a paved pathway to the nearby bathhouse, and barrier-free access to both sides. There's a roll-in shower with a hand-held showerhead and a fold-down shower bench in both the men's and women's bathhouses. Other access features include a small built-in shower bench, toilet grab bars and a roll-under sink on each side.

Resources

Myakka River State Park
(941) 361-6511
www.floridastateparks.org/park/Myakka-River

Cabin Reservations
(800) 326-3521
www.floridastateparks.reserveamerica.com

John Pennecamp Coral Reef State Park

H ome to the world's third largest coral reef, John Pennekamp Coral
Reef State Park encompasses 70 nautical square miles, and is located
near the beginning of the Overseas Highway across the Florida Keys. The
park is worthy of a visit just to enjoy the mangrove swamp and tropical
hammock vegetation, but it also gets a big thumbs-up for its wheelchair-
accessible water activities. So not only can wheelchair-users and slow
walkers hit the beach at this Key Largo park, but they can also hop on a
boat and explore some of the many underwater treasures of the coral reef.

Attractions

Visitor Center

The visitor center is located near the marina, and there's plenty of
accessible parking in the large adjacent lot. There's curb-cut access over
to the visitor center, with ramp access up to the front door. Inside, there's
level access to the information desk and interpretive exhibits, and barrier-
free access around the massive 30,000-gallon saltwater aquarium. Filled
with local reef residents, the aquarium includes a goldentail moray, a long-
spined urchin, sea anemones, nurse sharks and the very colorful sergeant

Picnic area near the concessions

major fish. It offers a good primer on local marine life and it's a must-see before you hit the glass bottom boat. There's also level access to the auditorium, which has wheelchair seating in back; and barrier-free access over to the accessible restrooms.

Concession Area

There's barrier-free access over to the concession area, which is located across the courtyard from the visitor center. The building features level access, with plenty of room to navigate a wheelchair inside. It includes a ticket counter for the glass bottom and dive boats, a gift shop, and a small food concession that sells ready made salads, sandwiches and pizza. There's also barrier-free access to the outdoor dining area behind the building (reserved for people who purchase food items inside), and level access over to the accessible picnic table.

A public picnic area is also available near the bathhouse. There's level access to a covered pavilion, which features a number of accessible tables on a cement pad. There are also several other smaller accessible picnic shelters located on the other side of the parking lot.

Boarding for the glass Bottom Boat

Bathhouse

There is ramp access up to the marina side of the bathhouse, which is located next to the concession area. There is an accessible shower outside with a fold-down shower bench. There are also accessible toilet stalls with grab bars and accessible changing areas inside. It should be noted that although the bathhouse has an accessible marina side entrance, there are steps up to it on the concession side.

Glass Bottom Boat

There's level access out to the boarding area for the *Spirit of Pennekamp*, with ramp access to the first deck of this glass bottom boat. Inside the main cabin there are two wheelchair spaces to view the marine life through the "windows" on the bottom of the boat. Ambulatory passengers can sit on one of the benches that line the windows, but you can get an equally good view from the wheelchair viewing area above them.

It takes about 45 minutes to travel out to the reef, and the boat spends about an hour out on the reef. During that time a marine biologist helps identify the fish that are visible through the bottom windows, and educates guests about the fragile marine ecosystem. It's an educational and informative tour, and you really never know what you'll see. It should also be noted that the on-board restrooms are tiny, and are not accessible; so plan ahead and use the accessible shore side facilities before boarding.

Snorkeling Excursion

Accessible snorkeling excursions are available on the *Encounter,* which features ramp access up to the boat, tie-downs and an accessible head. The 2.5-hour tour includes snorkeling equipment, instruction, and assistance getting in and out of the water. The boat has one large step down to the water at the aft end, and the usual procedure for wheelchair-users is to back the wheelchair up to the back of the boat, then transfer to the ground and scoot into the water. The captain is very experienced with wheelchair passengers, and his crew offers as much — or as little — assistance as required. The crew is well trained and they understand that every disability is different, and that not everyone requires, or even wants, the same degree of assistance. So, if you've always wanted to give snorkeling a try, and have at least some upper body strength, this may be a good option for you.

Kayaks

Tandem kayaks are available for rent at the marina, so folks with some upper body strength can explore the 50-mile natural mangrove wilderness in the park. The kayak ramp is wheelchair-accessible and there's excellent signage for the accessible paths of travel on the docks.

Far Beach

Far Beach is located a short drive from the marina, at the end of the park road. Accessible parking is located near the beach mats, which allow wheelchair access over the sand, and down to the water. A beach wheelchair is also available at the visitor center. A level boardwalk next to the beach mats leads over to accessible family restrooms and accessible outdoor showers. There's also barrier-free access to a small viewing platform on the other side of the restrooms.

Mangrove Trail

The Mangrove Trail is located across the parking lot from Far Beach. This .75-mile accessible boardwalk trail leads through a mangrove swamp; and allows visitors a closer look at the estuary ecosystem. There is an observation tower near the midway point of the boardwalk, but it is

Viewing Platform at Far Beach

only accessible by stairs. This trail was closed for repairs at press time, and no re-opening date was available. Check with the park office for the latest updates. There's also a small picnic area in the parking lot, with an accessible table on an asphalt pad.

Lodging

Campground

The campground is just a short drive from the marina and concession area, and it offers three accessible RV or trailer sites. Sites 38, 39 and 40 each have an accessible table, a grill and a cement driveway. The sites also feature an accessible path to the nearby bathhouse, which is equipped with a roll-in shower with a fold-down shower bench, grab bars and a hand-held shower head. There is also a small changing area with a bench next to the accessible shower.

Bathhouse at the campground

Nearby

Long Key State Park

Although Long Key State Park is about 56 miles away from John Pennekamp Coral Reef State Park, it's definitely worth a visit while you're in the neighborhood. Located at Mile Marker 37.5 on the Overseas Highway, the scenic drive there — down US Route 1, with the ocean literally lapping at the causeway — is nothing short of spectacular. And with plenty of spots to stop and enjoy the view, the drive is a destination in itself.

Long Key State Park is home to a healthy bird population, and although there aren't a lot of accessible features in this small park, the Golden Orb Trail is a good choice for wheelchair-users and slow walkers.

Accessible parking is available near the trailhead, with level access over to the accessible restrooms. The 1.25-mile trail begins as a boardwalk over a mangrove swamp, and then crosses a bridge and transitions into a sandy coastal berm. Although most wheelchair-users will have problems with the deep sand and exposed tree roots on the coastal berm, the boardwalk is nicely accessible.

Camping shelter on the Golden Orb Trail

For a longer hike, double back and then try the trail in reverse, beginning with the shaded rockland hammock section. Not only is this canopy of gumbo limbo trees a prime habitat for the white-crowned pigeon and the Key West quail dove, it also provides some welcome respite from the harsh midday sun. And although the trail is named for the large golden orb spider, I'm happy to report that I had no arachnid encounters along the way.

The popular beach campground at this park is usually filled to the brim with RVs, and even though it's one of the most coveted campgrounds in the Sunshine State, sadly there are no wheelchair-accessible sites. That said, if you don't mind roughing it a bit there are six primitive campsites located near the beginning of the Golden Orb Tail.

The covered shelters are connected by a level boardwalk, and they each have plenty of space for a tent. There's level access to all the shelters, and about half of them have wheelchair-accessible picnic tables. There's barrier-free access to the nearby outdoor showers and a shared community grill, and you just can't beat the ocean view. And unlike the higher priced beach campground, this secluded camping area isn't highly publicized. It's also not reservable through standard on-line channels, so contact the park directly for more information. Even if you can only stay one night, it's definitely worth the slight detour.

Resources

John Pennecamp Coral Reef State Park
(305) 451-1202
www.floridastateparks.org/park/Pennekamp
www.pennekamppark.com

Long Key State Park
(305) 664-4815
www.floridastateparks.org/park/Long-Key

Jonathan Dickinson State Park

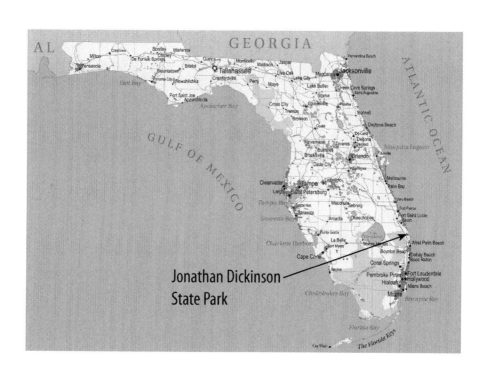

Jonathan Dickinson
State Park

L ocated on Florida's east coast, about 100 miles north of Miami, Jonathan Dickinson State Park is one of the state's largest and most diverse state parks. At over 10,500 acres the park supports 13 different ecosystems; and includes vegetation that ranges from sand pine scrub and pine flatwood, to mangrove swamps. And if that's not reason enough to visit, it's also home to a number of rare and endangered species. Top it off with a very comfortable accessible cabin, and you have all the makings for a great back-to-nature getaway.

Attractions

Elsa Kimbell Environmental Education and Research Center

The Elsa Kimbell Environmental Education and Research Center offers a good overview of the park's facilities. It's located near the end of the park road, just north of the River Campground. Accessible parking is available in the first lot, next to an accessible sidewalk that leads to the front door. Inside, there's barrier-free access to the interpretive exhibits and the small theater. The center is staffed with knowledgeable volunteers, and it also offers a good selection of interactive learning activities for children.

Picnic area near the River Store

River Area Facilities

A number of accessible park facilities are located in the river area, next door to the research center. There's accessible parking in the second parking lot, with barrier-free access over to an accessible picnic shelter with a grill. The sidewalk continues towards the river and leads to public restrooms which have accessible stalls and roll-under sinks. Accessible outdoor showers are also located near the restrooms.

There's a large picnic area under the trees near the river, with a few accessible tables near the sidewalk. The sidewalk runs along the river, and past the swimming area; however the swimming area is located down a grassy slope that lacks an accessible path.

There's level access to the River Store which is located next to the tour boat dock. The store sells groceries, drinks, snacks and souvenirs, as well as Trapper Nelson Boat Tour tickets. There's also barrier-free access to a small outdoor dining area behind the store.

A paved path leads from the store over to the amphitheater, which offers good wheelchair access and accessible seating near the back.

Trapper Nelson Boat Tour

Although the concessionaire has made the Trapper Nelson Boat Tour as

Boarding for the Trapper Nelson Boat Tour

accessible as possible, there are still some obstacles along the way, and participants can expect to take at least 12 steps on the tour. With that in mind, this tour is really only doable for some slow walkers and part-time wheelchair-users.

There are several tours during the day, most of which stop at Trapper John Nelson's site, which is located along the Loxahatchee River. Known as the Wildman of Loxahatchee, Nelson came to the area in the 1930s and lived off the land. He subsequently opened Trapper's Jungle Gardens and Wildlife Zoo at the site. It should be noted that not all cruises visit the site, as it's only accessible at high tide. Still, its a nice wildlife cruise, even without the stop.

There's level access to the tour boat dock, but there are two steps up to the boat. There's also a gap between the steps and the boat, and since there's no handrail, passengers with balance issues will definitely need assistance. Once aboard, wheelchair-users must transfer to a seat for the cruise.

The landing area at the Nelson site is very sandy, and passengers have to be able to step in and out of the boat to access it. A park ranger meets the boat and takes visitors on a short tour through the remnants of the zoo and gardens. Although the soil is firmer once you head inland, there are steps into some of the buildings. Still if you can manage the walk, it's a very interesting tour.

Even if you are unable to do the boat tour, be sure and take a stroll out on the dock. It features level access — so it's a good choice for everyone — and it offers a particularly scenic view of the Loxahatchee River.

Kitching Creek Nature Trail

The Kitching Creek Nature Trail is located near the river area facilities, at the far corner of the third parking lot. Accessible parking is located near the trail, with level access over to the trailhead.

This 1.25-mile ramble travels along Wilson Creek and through pine flatwoods to an overlook on Kitching Creek. Although the trail is wide and fairly level, it's probably a better choice for power wheelchair- and scooter-users, as some light sand and other obstacles may hinder most manual wheelchair-users.

The trail begins with a hard-packed dirt surface, and the first stretch is fairly accessible. There's a small lip on the bridge that crosses Wilson Creek, and after that there are patches of sand and a few tree roots along the trail. There's a one-inch lip up to the shaded overlook at Kitching Creek, and after that the palmetto-lined trail transitions back to a hard-packed dirt surface. Finally, the trail continues on through some grassy areas, crosses back over Wilson Creek, and leads out to the parking lot.

Alternatively, there's a shorter loop of the trail that may work for most people. Just make a left turn after you cross the first bridge on Wilson Creek, and follow the trail alongside the water. At the next bridge, cross back over the river, and complete the loop back out to the parking lot.

Give it a try, as you can always turn back if the access doesn't work for you. It should also be noted that wild hogs like this habitat, so you may find some holes along the trail. That said, the trail is pretty wide in most areas, so these obstacles are usually easy to dodge.

Bicycle Trail

There's no shortage of bicycle trails throughout the park, but the one-mile section of the multiuse trail that begins behind the research center is a good choice for wheelchair-users and slow walkers. This paved trail is wide and level, and it winds along the river and over to the Eagles View Trail. And if you can't manage the distance, a power wheelchair is available for loan at the entrance station.

The Kitching Creek Trail

Boat Ramp

A public boat ramp and pier are located at the end of the park road, just south of the River Campground. Accessible parking is located near the pier, and there's level access to the accessible picnic shelter that's next to the boat ramp. It's seldom very busy in this area of the park, so it's a good place to go for a quiet lunch.

Audio Driving Tour

A free audio driving tour is available at the entrance station or the research center. The CD and interpretive book contain information about 12 different sites in the park along the scenic 10 mile driving route. The audio tour offers a comprehensive history of the park and includes excerpts from the 1696 journal of Jonathan Dickinson. It also gives a good overview of the park's natural history, and its diverse ecosystems.. A sheet of QR codes is also available if you'd prefer to listen to the tour on a smart phone.

Gator Culvert

Gator Culvert, which is located midway between the entrance station and the river area, offers an accessible boardwalk and – if you're lucky – some gator viewing. There's no striped parking, but there's plenty of room to

Boardwalk to Gator Culvert

park parallel in the wide level area near the beginning of the boardwalk. There's level access to the boardwalk, and over to the viewing platform at the culvert. The trail is just 100 yards long, and there's also a bench to sit and enjoy the view at the end of the boardwalk.

Lodging

Cabin 3

Accessible cabin 3 is located near the River Campground, just east of the research center. There's accessible parking on a paved pad in front of the cabin, with a level sidewalk to the entrance in the back. Access features include wide doorways, wood floors and plenty of room to maneuver a wheelchair.

The large great room is furnished with a 12-inch high sleeper sofa and a 22-inch high open-frame queen-sized bed with wheelchair access on both sides. The kitchen area has a roll-under sink, a cooktop, a microwave, a toaster, a coffee pot and a small refrigerator; however it lacks a freezer or an oven. The cabinets are fully stocked with utensils, plates, glasses, pots and pans; and there's also a dining table with four chairs in the great room.

Cabin 3

The bathroom has a roll-in shower with grab bars, a hand-held showerhead and a fold down shower bench. It's very nicely designed, with a drain running the length of the shower to insure adequate drainage. The toilet grab bars are located on the back and right walls (as seated), and the bathroom also has a roll-under sink and an adjustable angled mirror. Add in some lowered hooks on the bathroom door, and you have a very accessible and usable setup.

Linens and towels are provided for the cabin, but make sure to bring soap and shampoo.

There's also level access out to the back patio, which is surrounded by palmettos for privacy. There's plenty of room to roll around on the patio which is equipped with an accessible picnic table, grill and a fire circle. It's a pleasant place to relax and enjoy Mother Nature.

Bathroom in Cabin 3

Sleeping area in Cabin 3

Living area in Cabin 3

Dining and kitchen areas in Cabin 3

River Campground

The River Campground is located near the end of the park road, and it features four accessible RV or tent sites.

Campsites 96, 106, 124, and 136 each have a paved driveway, a level area for a tent, and an accessible table and grill. There's also an accessible path to the bathhouses from these campsites. The bathhouses were remodeled in 2016, and they include accessible toilet stalls, roll-under sinks, and roll-in showers with grab bars and fold down shower benches.

Pine Grove Campground

The Pine Grove Campground is located near the entrance, and it features one accessible tent or RV site, and three RV or trailer sites.

Campsite 5, which is an accessible tent or RV site, is located in the first loop. It features a paved driveway, a level tent pad, and an accessible picnic table and grill. Campsites 9, 21 and 36 are also located in the first loop, but they are RV or trailer sites. These sites have the same access features as campsite 5, but they lack a level tent pad. Campsites 60 and 79 are located in the second loop, and these RV or trailer sites have the same access features as campsites 9, 21, and 36. There is also an accessible paved path to the bathhouses from all of the accessible campsites.

The bathhouses all feature a stall with an accessible toilet, a roll-under sink and a child seat with a seat belt. They also all have a 36-inch square roll-in shower with grab bars, a fold down shower bench and a lowered showerhead. A private changing area is located next to the shower.

Resources

Jonathan Dickinson State Park
(772) 546-2771
www.floridastateparks.org/park/Jonathan-Dickinson

Cabin Reservations
(800) 326-3521
www.floridastateparks.reserveamerica.com

Blue Spring State Park

Although this popular Florida state park is just 30 miles north of Orlando, it's a world away from the frenetic pace of the state's theme park capital. The namesake blue-green spring — the largest one on the St. Johns River — serves as a much needed refuge for West Indian Manatees during the winter months. The comfortable 72-degree water also offers a refuge for human visitors when the manatees are not in residence. Add in a barrier-free boardwalk trail, and one of the most accessible boat tours that I've ever seen, and you have a first-rate natural attraction.

Attractions

Upper Parking Area

There are two parking areas at the end of the park road near the spring. It should be noted that once the parking areas are full, the park closes its gates for the day. Best bet is to arrive early — especially during the busy summer months — to avoid disappointment.

The upper parking area, which is the first parking area past the Sand Pine Scrub Campground, offers access to a number of facilities. There's accessible parking next to a level sidewalk, which leads over to several accessible picnic shelters, as well as some individual accessible tables on a level area under the trees. Accessible restrooms are located near the picnic shelters, and there's also level access to the adjacent outside shower. The Camp Store is located near the picnic area, and it features level access and plenty of room to maneuver a wheelchair inside. It offers made-to-order deli sandwiches, drinks, ice cream and snacks. The gift shop, which is next door, also offers barrier-free access. Picnic tables with movable benches and a wheelchair-accessible gazebo are on a level cement area in front of the store.

The swimming area, which is across from the Camp Store, is usually open from April to mid-November, but park management may close it anytime they feel swimmers or manatees are in danger. There's ramp access down to the swimming area, but you need to be able to negotiate 10-12 steps to get into the water. Because of the clarity of the water, snorkeling is also a popular activity at this spring. Warning signs caution swimmers to watch for alligators, so proceeded with caution if you decide to enter the water.

Lower Parking Area

There's also plenty of accessible parking in the lower parking area, which is located down the road. There's level access from the parking area over to the dock, where visitors can purchase tickets for a St. Johns River Cruise or a Segway Tour. Accessible picnic tables and restrooms are located a short level roll from the parking area, and there's also ramped access to the kayak rental stand near the dock.

The Thursby House, which is located a short walk from the dock, is also worth a visit. Louis P. Thursby, who constructed one of the first steamboat landings on the St. Johns River, built this wood frame home for his family in 1872. There's ramp access to the back porch, level access to the front door, and barrier-free access throughout the first-floor of this three-story home. Visitors are invited to enjoy a self-guided tour of the first floor whenever the home is open; however the hours were limited at press time. Even if it's not open, it's still worth a stop to have a look at the outside of this historic house.

Boardwalk Trail

An accessible boardwalk trail begins at the dock and follows the St. Johns River through the mangroves up to the boil — or origin — of the spring.

Boardwalk trail

It's a shady level walk, and there are plenty of benches spaced out along the third-mile route. Several overlooks are located along the boardwalk, which transitions into a sidewalk when it passes the concession area near the upper parking area. The trail returns to a boardwalk at the gift shop and ends at a viewing platform, where you'll likely spot some manatees from mid-November through March. If you'd prefer a shorter walk, then park in the upper parking area and pick up the boardwalk trail at the gift shop.

St Johns River Cruise

Don't miss the excellent St. Johns River Cruise, which departs from the dock near the lower parking area. The two-hour tour travels along eight miles of the St. Johns River and circles two islands. Along the way a naturalist points out the wildlife, and moves in for a closer look whenever possible. The *Native II* was created for shallow water, so it's possible to get pretty close to shore; and since the engine is quiet it doesn't spook the wildlife.

There's level access to the dock, and several steps up to the boat; however lift access is available for folks that can't manage the steps. The former Amtrak lift is a mechanical lift, so it's not dependent on a power source and it's very easy to use. As a result, wheelchair-users can board the boat easily in both high and low tides.

A view of a manatee and her calf from the boardwalk trail

The average cruising speed of the boat is a very mild six mph, and wheelchair-users can stay in their wheelchair or transfer to a seat. The head has a wide door, but because the toilet is on a pedestal, it's about 36 inches high. Best bet is to use the accessible restroom on shore before boarding.

Expect to see white-tailed deer, turkeys, herons, and lots of gators on the tour. Be on the lookout for trails of circular bubbles too, as that usually indicates the presence of manatees. The naturalist has a good eye for spotting these, and if you're lucky you may even catch a glimpse of these magnificent animals when they surface for air.

The morning cruises are usually less crowded, and the animals are also more active earlier in the day. And if you want a discount on your cruise ticket, make your reservation on-line. You don't have to pay for the tickets until you pick them up, and an advance reservation also guarantees you a seat on the cruise, which usually sells out during the peak season.

Segway Tours

Slow Walkers may also want to try one of the Segway Tours that are offered by the St. Johns River Cruise folks. Participants need to be able to stand up and maintain their balance in order to take the guided tours, which are conducted on Segway All Terrain X2 transporters. Tryout

Boarding ramp for the St. Johns River Cruise

sessions — which are credited to the full tour price — are also available for folks who are unsure if the tour will work for them.

The two-hour tours include complete training, safety gear and a practice session in the parking lot. The guided tours, which travel along part of the Pine Island Hiking Trail, include lots of photo stops along the way. No prior Segway experience is needed, and all tours require a minimum of two participants. Reservations for the tours must be made at least 24 hours in advance.

Pine Island Hiking Trail

The Pine Island Hiking Trail begins in the lower parking area; and although this 3.6-mile trail is not rated as accessible, the first section may be doable for some slow walkers. Accessible parking is located near the trailhead, and the trail begins as a wide level hard-packed dirt path through a shaded cabbage palm hammock. A bench is located at about the half-mile point, after which the trail opens up to a pine forest and the soil becomes lightly sandy. As the trail continues the sand gets deeper and deeper, until it becomes impossible to move forward in a wheelchair. Still the shaded hammock makes for a nice one-mile out-and-back hike.

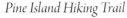

Pine Island Hiking Trail

Lodging

Cabin 2

Cabin 2 is an accessible cabin that's located a short walk away from the spring. This two-bedroom cabin features accessible parking next to the ramped entrance up to the screen porch, and level access to the wide front door.

The living room is furnished with a 12-inch high king-sized sleeper sofa, with wheelchair access on the left side (as you face it), a love seat, coffee table and end tables. A gas fireplace graces once side of the room, and a dining table with four chairs sits next to the kitchen. The fully equipped kitchen includes a stove, oven, dishwasher, full-size refrigerator and freezer, two microwaves, and a coffee pot. There's also a full contingent of plates, cups, glasses, utensils and pots and pans, so you can whip up everything from a frozen pizza to a gourmet dinner.

One bedroom is furnished with two 25-inch high twin beds with an access aisle between them, and a chest of drawers. The other bedroom has a 25-inch high double bed with wheelchair access on the right side (as you face it), a chest of drawers and a nightstand. Because of the placement of the chest of drawers, this bedroom only has 32 inches of clear space near the doorway, so it might be a tight fit for some folks.

Cabin 2

The bathroom has a 36-inch square roll-in shower with a slight one-inch lip; and because of the placement of the floor mounted toilet grab bar there's only 26 inches of clearance space at the entry. The shower is equipped with grab bars, a hand-held showerhead, and a portable shower bench. The floor mounted toilet grab bar is located on the right side (as seated), and there's also a standard wall mounted grab bar on the back wall. There's ample room to roll up to the toilet for a lateral transfer on one side, and the bathroom also has a roll-under sink and an angled mirror.

Towels and linens are provide in this cabin, but guests must supply their own soap and shampoo.

The spacious screen porch has an accessible picnic table and three rocking chairs, and there's also an accessible picnic table on a dirt pad in front of the cabin. A grill and a fire ring are located near the table. Wild pigs seem to favor the vegetation around the house, but they are easily spooked by people. Still, if you sit quietly on the screen porch in the late afternoon, you'll probably get a good look at them.

Because of the tight space in the bedrooms and the narrow transfer space into the shower, this cabin is best suited for slow walkers or part-time wheelchair-users who are able to walk a few steps.

One of the best features of the cabin is that it's very private because of the surrounding vegetation, and with just six cabins in the loop it's also very quiet.

Bedroom in Cabin 2

Living room in Cabin 2

Kitchen and dining areas in Cabin 2

Bathroom in Cabin 2

Sand Pine Scrub Campground

The Sand Pine Scrub Campground is located near the park entrance and it has five accessible tent or RV sites. Campsites 6, 7, 15, 16 and 41 each have a paved driveway, a level tent pad, an accessible picnic table, a grill and a fire ring. Additionally they all have a paved pathway to the nearby bathhouses.

Campsites 6, 7 and 41 are located close to the men's and women's bathhouses. Both sides feature level access and include a roll-in shower with a hand held-showerhead, an accessible toilet stall and a roll-under sink.

Campsites 15 and 16 are close to the accessible family shower room, which includes a roll-in shower with a hand-held showerhead, a toilet with grab bars on the right and back walls (as seated), and a roll-under sink. It's a very spacious and accessible room, with plenty of space to maneuver even the largest wheelchair or scooter.

Resources

Blue Spring State Park
(386) 775-3663
www.floridastateparks.org/park/Blue-Spring

St. Johns River Cruises
(407) 330-1612
www.sjrivercruises.com

Cabin Reservations
(800) 326-3521
www.floridastateparks.reserveamerica.com

Wekiwa Springs State Park

Although it's not as large as some of Florida's other state parks, Wekiwa Springs is definitely worth a visit — especially for wheelchair-users. The crystal clear water stays a very comfortable 72 degrees year round, and wheelers and slow walkers can do more than just sit back and admire its beauty. Thanks to a wheelchair lift, everyone can access this second-magnitude spring, and swim, snorkel or just enjoy the water. There's also a wide variety of wildlife in the forest around the spring at this Orlando area park, and even a nice boardwalk trail through a hardwood hammock. And how can you pass up a park where the rangers actually put out bowls of water for the wild turkeys?

Attractions

Upper Boardwalk

It's just a short drive to the main parking lot from the entrance station, but it's best to arrive early in the day, as park gates close when the lot is full. Peak visitation occurs during the summer months, especially on weekends, so plan ahead. For best access to the springs, park in the first lot. There's

Upper boardwalk to the springs

plenty of accessible parking near a wide level boardwalk which leads down to the springs.

Restrooms and changing areas are located mid-way along the boardwalk. There's level access to the restrooms, which have accessible stalls and roll-under sinks; however the changing areas are not accessible. That said, the stalls are quite spacious, with plenty of room to change into a bathing suit.

The boardwalk continues down to a sidewalk which runs alongside the springs. There's an accessible picnic table under a tree to the left of the sidewalk; and although you can get a great view of the springs from this point, the accessible entrance is located over near the concession area. There's barrier-free access to the small nature center, which is about halfway between the accessible picnic table and the concession area. The kiosk offers wildlife exhibits and a video, and has plenty of room for wheelchair-users. The adjacent pavilion — where interpretive programs are held — has level access and wheelchair seating in a level cement area.

Concession Area

The concession area is located at the end of the sidewalk, a short walk from the nature center. Although there are a few paths down to the springs from

Wheelchair lift at the speings

the sidewalk, they all have steps along the way.

There's level access to the Camp Store, which offers some grocery items, and has a small snack bar and a kayak rental desk. The adjacent patio has accessible seating in a shady area. Free lockers (bring your own lock) are located just off the patio, but there's a step up to them. There's also another set of accessible restrooms behind the store.

Lower Boardwalk

A second boardwalk trail leads from the patio down to the springs. There's level access to this wide trail, which has several switchbacks along the way, as it gently descends down through the surrounding forest. This is the only accessible way to get down to the springs, and at just 300 feet long it's a very doable stroll.

Wekiwa Springs

By far the main attraction at this park is the water itself, which flows out into the Wekiva River at a rate of forty-two million gallons per day. There's an accessible sidewalk that leads past a level beach area, over a bridge and around the springs. A fixed wheelchair lift is located next to the water, near the end of the lower boardwalk. The lift is kept locked, so if you plan to use

Wet to Dry Trail

it, inquire at the entrance station before you head down to the springs.

Canoe Beach

An accessible boardwalk to the right of the wheelchair lift leads out to Canoe Beach. There are three steps down to the canoe dock; however kayaks are launched directly from the hard-packed dirt beach. Tandem kayaks are available for rent, but because of the launch setup, kayaking is really only a viable option for slow walkers. Still, take the time to walk over to the dock for a nice view of the Wekiva River.

Wet to Dry Trail

The one-mile Wet to Dry Trail begins on the opposite side of the springs, across the water from the wheelchair lift and the lower boardwalk. The trail travels through three different communities, and begins as a boardwalk through a hardwood forest hammock. The wide boardwalk is mostly level and features low bumpers instead of a railing, so wheelchair-users have a full view of the surrounding forest. There are also several benches along the way for slow walkers to take a break.

About halfway along the way, the trail transitions to a hard-packed dirt trail, and although it starts out fine, it slowly becomes littered with

Wekiwa Springs swimming area

96

more and more tree roots, until it's not at all accessible. So do as much of it as you can, and double back. On the plus side, you'll get an entirely different view on the way back.

Picnic Area

A dirt path leads from the concession area down to the picnic area, but it's bumpy, has a steep grade, and it's not wheelchair-accessible. Alternatively, the picnic area can be accessed from the third parking lot, which features accessible parking and level access over to the Live Oak Pavilion. This picnic shelter has an accessible table and plenty of room to maneuver a wheelchair. If the shelter is occupied, there are also a few standard picnic tables on firm ground close to the restroom; however most of the tables near the picnic shelter are on sandy soil.

There's a sidewalk that leads from the picnic shelter to the restroom, but because of the grade most manual wheelchair-users will need some assistance. The restroom itself is accessible, with a very large accessible stall and roll-under sinks.

There's also level access to the nearby playground, which is covered in wood chips.

Covered picnic area at Wekiwa Springs

Lodging

Sandhill Campground

The Sandhill Campground is located near the springs, and it features two accessible tent or RV campsites.

Campsites 2 and 60 are classified as accessible, but in truth campsite 2 is the only one that will work for wheelchair-users. Both sites have a level tent pad, and while campsite 2 has an accessible picnic table, campsite 60 has a standard one. The sites are close to different bathhouses. There's a level sidewalk to the bathhouse from campsite 2; however there is a step up to the sidewalk from campsite 60. The bathhouses both have level access, an accessible stall, roll-under sinks and an accessible shower area.

Resources

Wekiwa Springs State Park
(407) 884-2009
www.floridastateparks.org/park/Wekiwa-Springs

Suwannee River State Park

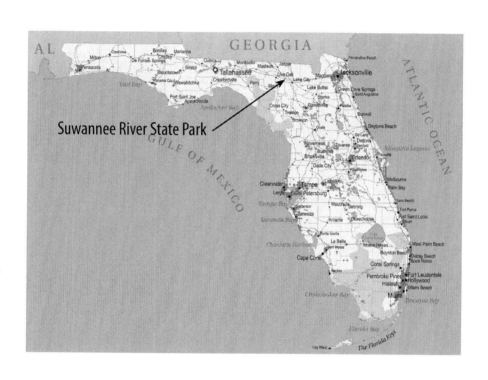

Suwannee River State Park

Located about 85 miles west of Jacksonville, Suwannee River State Park offers a glimpse into the past as well as a taste of the "Real Florida". From a Civil War Cemetery and some historic earthen forts, to the namesake river that gently meanders alongside Spanish moss-draped oaks, this park tops the list as far as diversity is concerned. Add in a very comfortable accessible cabin — one that has all the homey touches of grandma's house — and you have a space where you can relax, unwind and enjoy the stunning natural beauty that Stephen Foster raved about in *Old Folks at Home.* And if that's not enough, the fireflies put on a pretty impressive show during the warmer months.

Attractions

Main Parking Area

The main parking area, which is located halfway between the entrance station and the campground, offers visitors access to the trails and picnic areas in the park.

There's plenty of accessible parking in this parking area, and although there's level access over to the facilities on the right, the picnic shelter and

Picnic area and playground at Suwannee River State Park

restrooms are not accessible. There are steps up to the shelter and the restrooms, and the accessible stalls are only 30 inches wide. Additionally, the women's accessible stall was "out of order" at press time. There is however one accessible picnic table on hard-packed dirt near the picnic shelter.

The facilities to the left of the parking area are much more accessible. There's level access to the picnic shelter, and the restrooms have usable accessible stalls. There's also level access to the playground, which is covered with wood chips; with several benches located nearby on a hard-packed dirt area.

Sandhill Trail

The Sandhill Trail, which begins across the parking lot from the accessible picnic shelter, may be doable for some power wheelchair- and scooter-users. The .8-mile loop begins at the bridge, and although the first 10-15 feet are dotted with ruts and tree roots, that's truly the most inaccessible portion of the trail.

After the first rough section, the trail opens up to a wide hard-packed dirt trail covered with forest duff and dotted with tree roots here and there. After the trail crosses the service road there are a few sandy patches, before it returns to hard-packed dirt.

Sandhill Trail at Suwannee River State Park

About half way along, the trail passes through the old Columbus Cemetery, which dates back to the Civil War. Most of the graves are fenced off, but there's level access around them on grass and hard-packed dirt paths. The cemetery contains historic and recent graves, with the last person being buried there in 1973.

After that the trail continues through the forest on a hard-packed dirt trail, and loops back to the parking lot. It's a pleasant stroll though a pine oak forest dotted with ferns, and the cemetery is must-do for history buffs.

Earthworks Overlook

The park also includes some earthen forts from the civil war. These long dirt mounds were built by confederate soldiers so they could defend the Suwannee River railroad bridge from union gunboats. Today a boardwalk leads out over one of the earthworks, and offers visitors a great river view.

The path out to the boardwalk begins directly across from the accessible picnic shelter — just look for the collection of old steamboat parts and follow the hard-packed dirt trail through the forest to the boardwalk. There are a few exposed roots in the forest, but the trail is pretty manageable for most folks. There's level access to the accessible boardwalk, which leads out to an overlook where visitors can get a good

Earthworks Overlook

view of the confluence of the Withlacoochee and Suwanee Rivers. There's also a level path around the earthwork, if you'd like a closer look at the walls of the earthen fort. At just a half-mile round-trip, this is the most accessible trail in the park.

Suwannee River Trail

Although the entire .8-mile length of the Suwannee River Trail is not accessible, the first portion may be doable for some wheelchair-users and slow walkers. The trail begins in the main parking area, and continues north past the inaccessible picnic shelter alongside the river. This hard-packed dirt trail is level, and although there are a few tree roots along the first section, they are easy to dodge.

The trail continues on through the oak forest and crosses the park road near the boat launch. After that a level bridge leads out across the Lime Sink Run; however the trail loses its access after that point. All in all it's about a half-mile round-trip stroll through the shaded forest, and it's definitely worth a try.

To bypass the roots on the first section of the trail, follow the paved park road to the boat launch, then turn right on the Suwanee River Trail and head over to the bridge. It's about the same distance as the riverside

Suwannee River Trail

trail, but it's a much smoother route. Alternatively you can take the riverside trail one way, and return on the park road.

And although this trail offers a good opportunity for a close look at the river, it's usually underwater after a heavy rain.

Lodging

Cabin 5

Cabin 5 is an accessible cabin that's located close to the campground. Accessible parking is available in front, near a ramp which leads up to the screened porch. There's level access to the cabin through the wide front door, which has a keypad entry. Inside, there's good pathway access throughout the unit, which has laminate floors for easy rolling.

The large great room is furnished with a love seat, an end table, a 13-inch high sleeper sofa and a gas fireplace. A dining table with four chairs is located next to a lowered bar with three chairs, and there's plenty of room to roll around the spacious dining area.

The spacious kitchen includes a cooktop, a gas oven, a dishwasher, a microwave and a full size refrigerator-freezer with ice and water in the door.

Cabin 5 at Suwannee River State Park

It also has a good selection of dishes, utensils and pots and pans. Access features include a roll-under sink, and level access out to the screened porch via a wide kitchen door.

One bedroom is furnished with a 28-inch high open-frame queen-sized bed with wheelchair access on both sides, two night tables and includes a closet with a lowered rod. This room also has private access out to the screened porch. The second bedroom has two 21-inch high open-frame twin beds with an access aisle in the middle. There is also wheelchair access on the left side of one of the beds (as you face it), but the other bed is pushed up against the wall. Other furnishings include a night table and a chest of drawers. The room also has a closet with a lowered rod.

The large bathroom includes a full five-foot turning radius, and is equipped with a tub/shower combination with grab bars, a hand-held showerhead and a fold-down shower bench. The toilet grab bars are located on the back and right walls (as seated), and the bathroom also includes a roll-under sink and a lowered mirror.

And don't miss the very accessible screened porch which wraps around the cabin and sports two rocking chairs, a swing and an accessible picnic table. There's also ramp access out to a back patio area where there's another accessible picnic table, a grill and a fire ring. It's the perfect place

Great room in Cabin 5

to watch the firefly show at night.

Best of all, there are a lot of personal touches – such as handmade quilts and vintage photos — incorporated into the interior decor of this cabin. It doesn't feel like a rental at all, and that's a very good thing.

Kitchen in Cabin 5

Bedroom with queen-sized bed in Cabin 5

Bedroom with twin beds in Cabin 5

Bathroom in Cabin 5

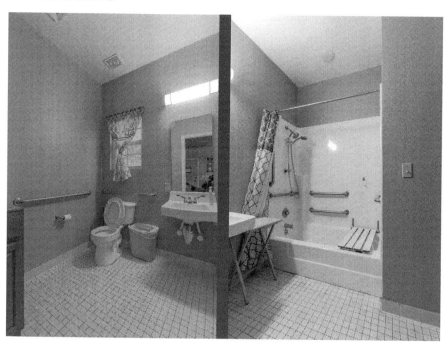

Screened porch at Cabin 5

Campground

The campground is located between the main parking area and the cabins. It has two accessible tent or RV sites, and one accessible RV or trailer site. Campsite 2 and campsite 3 are accessible tent or RV sites, and they each have a paved driveway, a level tent space, an accessible picnic table and a fire circle. Campsite 27 is an accessible RV or trailer site, and it features a paved driveway, an accessible picnic table and a fire circle.

It should be noted that campsites 2 and 3 are sometimes taken out of inventory for use by the campground hosts.

There's a paved level pathway from all of the accessible sites to the bathhouse; however campsite 27 is the closest one to the facility. The bathhouse features level access to a private room with an accessible toilet stall and a roll-under sink. The spacious room is also equipped with a roll-in shower with grab bars, a hand-held showerhead and a fold-down shower bench. It's very nicely done access-wise, with room for even the largest wheelchair and an attendant.

Nearby

Wes Skyles Peacock Springs State Park

Wes Skyles Peacock Springs State Park, which is located just 40 minutes from Suwannee River State Park at the opposite end of Live Oak, is also worth a visit while you're in the area. This small park boasts two major springs and it's a favorite for cave divers. That said, its also a good place to enjoy the natural beauty, and it's the perfect spot for a quiet picnic lunch. Plus, the drive there is very scenic.

The one down side to this park is that it doesn't have any paved roads. That said, even though the one-lane park road is a bit bumpy, it's still manageable in a low clearance vehicle if you take it slow. There's no manned entrance station or information booth, so just follow the signs down the main park road to the springs.

The hard-packed dirt parking area near the springs is level, and there's lots of room to parallel park for ramp or lift access. There are also a few standard picnic tables near the parking area that are usable; however the nearby porta potty is not wheelchair-accessible.

There's level access over to the boardwalk which leads about 100

Boardwalk to Peacock Springs

yards through a native maple stand to the cypress lined springs. In order to access the springs you need to descend four steps, but you can still get a good view from the end of the boardwalk.

The Orange Grove Picnic Area is a nice choice for a quiet lunch break. It's located near the entrance, and although there's no accessible parking, there's still room to parallel park there as well. There's a short hard-packed path to the picnic shelter, which has a slight lip, and barrier-free access over to a standard picnic table that's under a massive maple tree. There are also a few standard picnic tables near the parking area if you can't manage the walk. Best of all, a level sidewalk leads from the parking area over to an accessible porta potty.

Despite some access obstacles this park is definitely worth the visit, as it's quite scenic, and you'll likely have it all to yourself while the divers explore the springs.

Resources

Suwannee River State Park
(386) 362-2746
www.floridastateparks.org/park/Suwannee-River

Wes Skyles Peacock Springs State Park
(386) 776-2194
www.floridastateparks.org/park/Peacock-Springs

Cabin Reservations
(800) 326-3521
www.floridastateparks.reserveamerica.com

22 Accessible Road Trips
Driving Vacations
FOR WHEELERS AND SLOW WALKERS

By Candy B. Harrington

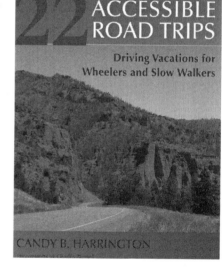

Billed as the world's first inclusive road trip book, this detailed resource features 22 driving routes across the United States, with information about wheelchair-accessible sites, lodging options, trails, attractions and restaurants along the way. A great read for anyone who wants to hit the road — disabled or able-bodied — *22 Accessible Road Trips* captures the diversity of America, with off-the-beaten-path finds and unique roadside attractions, as well as must-see metropolitan sights in the gateway cities.

www.22AccessibleRoadTrips.com

Barrier-Free Utah
Utah National Parks
FOR WHEELERS AND SLOW WALKERS

By Candy B. Harrington

This handy guide includes detailed information about accessible trails, sites, lodging options, tours, transportation and attractions in Zion, Bryce Canyon, Capitol Reef, Arches and Canyonlands National Parks. Along with detailed information about trails and viewpoints that will work for wheelchair-users and slow walkers, it also includes detailed descriptions of all the in-park lodging options, along with photographs of the accessible rooms. Access details and photos of 23 additional accessible lodging options near the parks are also included, as well as information on accessible campsites in the parks.

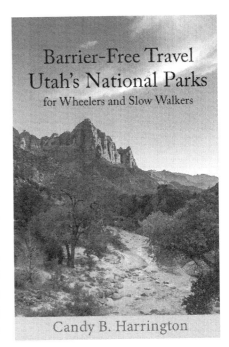

Top it off with information about ranger-led tours, loaner wheelchairs and the free America the Beautiful Access Pass and you have a very comprehensive resource.

www.barrierfreeutah.com

113

47636605R00070

Made in the USA
Middletown, DE
29 August 2017